ANIMAL WISE

Pointy, Long, or Round

A Book About Animal Shapes

by Patricia M. Stockland
illustrated by Todd Ouren

Special thanks to our advisers for their expertise:

Zoological Society of San Diego
San Diego Zoo
San Diego, California

Susan Kesselring, M.A., Literacy Educator
Rosemount-Apple Valley-Eagan (Minnesota) School District

PICTURE WINDOW BOOKS
Minneapolis, Minnesota

Managing Editor: Catherine Neitge
Creative Director: Terri Foley
Art Director: Keith Griffin
Editor: Christianne Jones
Designer: Todd Ouren
Page production: Picture Window Books
The illustrations in this book were prepared digitally.

Picture Window Books
5115 Excelsior Boulevard
Suite 232
Minneapolis, MN 55416
877-845-8392
www.picturewindowbooks.com

Printed in the United States of America.

Library of Congress Cataloging-in-Publication Data
Stockland, Patricia M.
Pointy, long, or round : a book about animal shapes /
by Patricia M. Stockland ; illustrated by Todd Ouren.
p. cm. — (Animal wise)
Includes bibliographical references (p.   ).
ISBN 1-4048-0935-X (hardcover)
1. Animals—Juvenile literature. 2. Shapes—Juvenile literature.
I. Ouren, Todd, ill. II. Title.

QL49.S775 2004
590—dc22   2004023306

Shape Adaptations

Sometimes being long or round can help an animal survive. Different shapes are one way that animals adapt.

Some animals have spiky shapes to protect them from predators. Others are long and lean so they can reach their food.

Find out how some animals use their shape to help them survive.

North American Porcupine

Spiky, needle-sharp points shake in the tree. A porcupine rests in the leaves.

This strangely shaped rodent is prickly for protection. Porcupines use their sharp quills to frighten predators. Bigger animals such as mountain lions stay away to keep from getting poked.

Porcupines can rattle their quills. This sound is another way of warning predators to stay away.

Walking Stick

A thin, brown stick hangs from a tree branch. Wait, that's not a stick. It's an insect!

A walking stick uses its long, thin body to blend in with sticks and leaves. Its brownish green color and skinny shape help the bug look like a twig so birds and reptiles don't eat it.

Walking sticks usually hide during the day and eat at night.

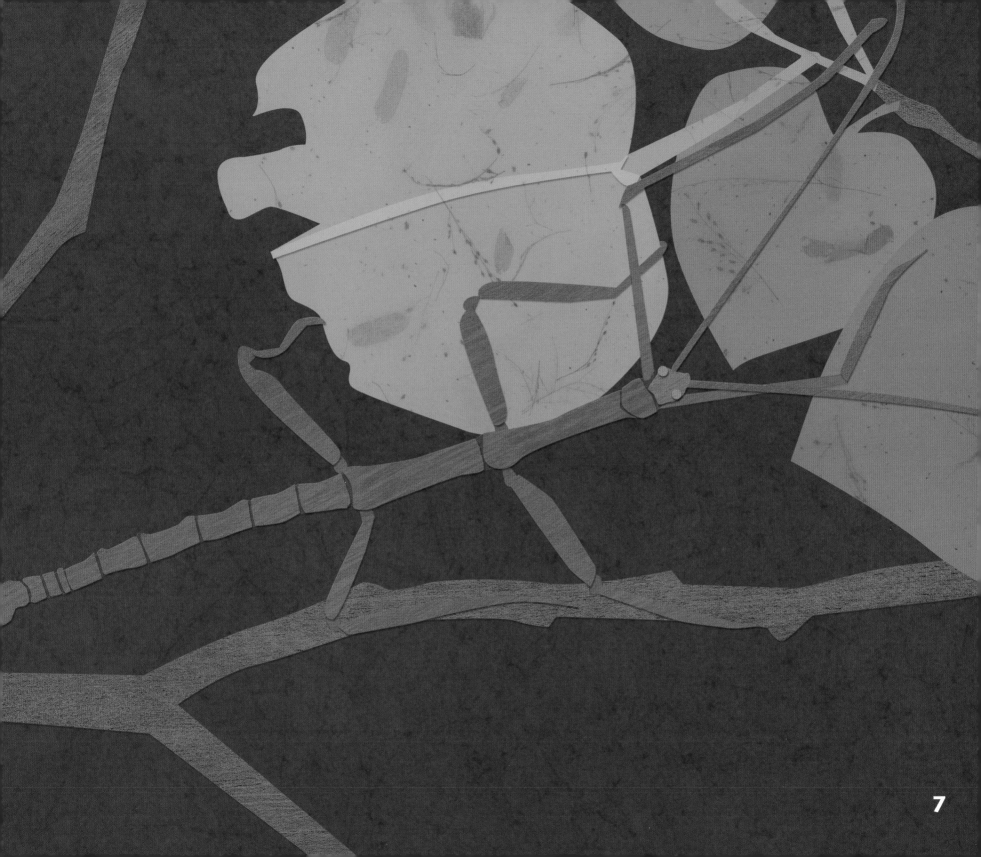

Flamingo

Long legs stand tall in the lagoon. The flamingo dips its head to feed.

This big bird has some crazy curves. Its bill is upside down. When a flamingo sticks its head in the water, the funny bill becomes a great scoop for food. Yum!

Flamingos pump mud and water through their bills. Food gets trapped in the edges of the bill, but the mud and water squirt out.

Scorpion

A strange creature with sharp claws and a curvy tail walks across the cool sand. Nighttime is suppertime for the scorpion.

The scorpion has claws like a crab. Insects, spiders, and mice get crushed in its claws. Scorpions also have a curved tail that ends with a stinger. Predators learn to steer clear of the scorpion's tail.

The venom of a tiny scorpion can be stronger than the venom of a big one.

Giraffe

A happy head pokes through the trees.
The long-necked giraffe munches on leaves.

Giraffes are the tallest animals alive today. Their long, slender necks help the creatures reach food in high places. When the savanna is hot and dry, giraffes can still reach leaves in the treetops.

Female giraffes feed on the lower branches. Male giraffes feed on the higher branches. By doing this, everyone gets plenty to eat.

Spiny Puffer Fish

Spikes cover this round, bobbing ball. The spiny puffer fish prepares for attack.

The spiny puffer isn't attacking anyone, though. It is keeping itself safe from the attack of predators. When this fish is afraid, it quickly swallows lots of water. The water puffs up the fish until it is round and hard. Then its spines stick out.

Once a puffer fish inflates itself, it moves at about half its normal speed. It's safe, though, because predators have a hard time getting their mouths around the spiky fish.

Leafy Sea Dragon

Seaweed floats in the water. But wait—that seaweed is actually a sea dragon.

The leafy sea dragon uses its strange shape to hide from prey. The fins on its body act as camouflage. Hungry fish don't notice the sea dragon swimming among the weeds on the reef.

The leafy sea dragon has leaflike parts that are connected to its body. That's why it can hide so well.

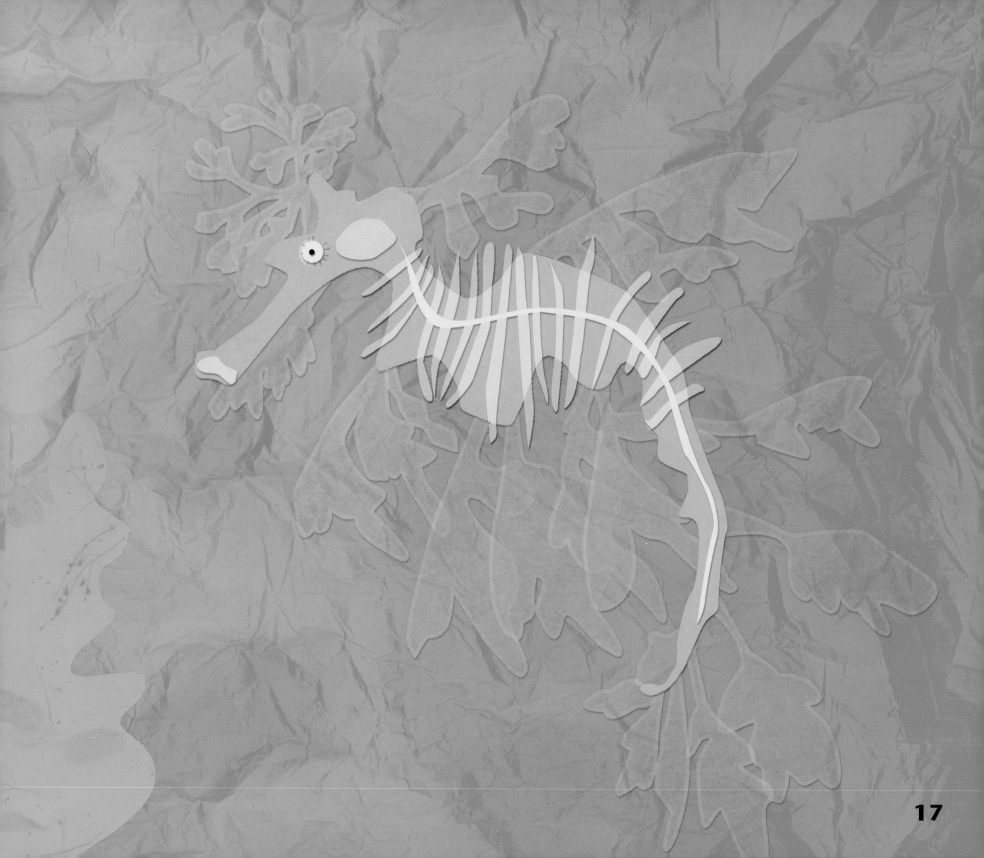

Mongoose

A long, lean shape moves through the grass. The stretched-out mongoose spies its prey.

This animal's sleek body helps it move quickly. Speed is a handy skill for a mongoose, especially when hunting snakes. Moving quickly keeps the mongoose from getting bitten by its own dinner.

Mongooses are related to cats and hyenas.

Platypus

It has a bill like a duck's and a tail like a beaver's. What is this strangely shaped creature?

The platypus is a mammal made of mismatched shapes. Those shapes all work together to help this animal find food. The platypus uses its bill to sense prey. Its webbed feet help it dive deep. Its funny tail stores fat for extra energy.

Platypuses have thick, waterproof fur that is perfect for swimming.

Do You Remember?

Point to the picture of the animal described in each question.

1. My skinny, brown body looks like part of a tree branch. Who am I?

   (walking stick)

2. If you frighten me, I'll puff up. Watch out for my spines! Who am I?

   (spiny puffer fish)

3. My curved bill might look funny, but it makes a great scoop. Who am I?

   (flamingo)

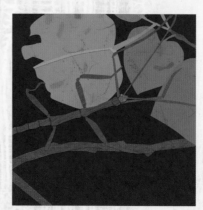

Fun Facts

A porcupine can have 30,000 quills covering its back.

To protect themselves from predators, some walking sticks will sway
as if they are blowing in the breeze.

Flamingos' diets are high in carotene. Carotene is found in the leaves they eat.
If the birds don't get enough carotene, they turn white.

Giraffes have only seven neck bones. That's the same number as humans.

To look bigger to its prey, the mongoose will stand on its hind legs
and stretch itself out to full height.

Glossary

camouflage—a disguise that keeps an animal from being seen, or markings
that make an animal look like something other than itself

fin—a flap sticking out from an animal's body that helps it move through water

lagoon—a body of water that is not very deep

predator—an animal that hunts and eats other animals

prey—an animal that is hunted by another animal for food

quills— hard hairs that are sharp and hollow

savanna— a grassy plain with only a few trees

venom—a poisonous liquid

TO LEARN MORE

At the Library

Berge, Claire. *Whose Shadow Is This? A Look at Animal Shapes—Round, Long, and Pointy.*
Minneapolis: Picture Window Books, 2004.

Petty, Kate. *Animal Camouflage and Defense.* Philadelphia: Chelsea House Publishers, 2004.

Whitehouse, Patricia. *Hiding in the Ocean.* Chicago: Heinemann Library, 2003.

On the Web

FactHound offers a safe, fun way to find Web sites related to this book.
All of the sites on FactHound have been researched by our staff.

1. Visit *www.facthound.com*
2. Type in this special code: 140480935X
3. Click the FETCH IT button.

our trusty FactHound will fetch the best Web sites for you!

DEX

all of the books in the Animal Wise series:

Round
imal Shapes

Feathers
imal Colors

Sand, Leaf, or Coral Reef
A Book About Animal Habitats

Strange Dances and Long Flights
A Book About Animal Behavior

Stripes, Spots, or Diamonds
A Book About Animal Patterns

Swing, Slither, or Swim
A Book About Animal Movements